EXTRAORDINARY MILLIONAIRE

Investment Tactics And Advice On How To Build And Preserve Wealth

BY

WILLIAMS P. HUGGINS

TABLE OF CONTENT

INTRODUCTION

W developing the proper mindset at the beginning of "Extraordinary Millionaire: Investment Tactics and Advice on How to Build and Preserve Wealth," we laid the foundation for the entire book. The phrase "Extraordinary Millionaire," which goes beyond the traditional definition of a millionaire, is introduced. In addition to having amassed a substantial fortune, an extraordinary millionaire is someone who has succeeded financially by combining strategic thought, self-discipline, and a distinct type of thinking.

Belief's Potency: The first step to becoming financially successful, we stress, is having faith in your ability to accumulate wealth. Your belief in yourself can be a strong incentive to take the required steps to achieve your financial objectives. The notion known as "The Power of Belief" highlights the significant influence beliefs may have on a variety of elements of our lives, from our capacity for achievement to our level of personal well-being. Perception, attitudes, and behaviors are shaped by our underlying cognitive and emotional states or beliefs. We will discuss this strong force's significance and ramifications in more detail here.

Self-confidence is based on one's belief in oneself. People are more willing to take chances, set high standards, and stick with something when things become difficult when they have a strong belief in their power. Personal development and accomplishment may be fueled by this self-assurance. Both our mental and physical health can benefit from the power of belief. Psychoneuroimmunology research indicates that our ideas affect our immune system and the state of our health in general. The placebo effect, for instance, shows how, even in cases where a treatment is ineffective, having faith in its effectiveness can result in noticeable improvements in health. People can develop resilience in the face of hardship by doing this. A more positive coping strategy that promotes emotional resilience and adaptation can result from the belief that setbacks are transitory and manageable. To achieve one's goals, one must have belief. Individuals are more likely to create specific objectives, maintain motivation, and persevere in their efforts when they have faith in their ability to fulfill their dreams. Because it frequently inspires the right behaviors and approaches to success, this idea has the potential to become self-fulfilling. On the one hand, empowering beliefs can come from negative or restrictive ones. These attitudes may operate as walls that one puts up to impede one's development as well as that of their career. To fully realize one's potential, it is imperative to identify and confront these limiting beliefs. Scientific, technological, and artistic advancements may be fueled by the potential for innovation and creativity. The possibility of novel ideas and pushing the envelope of what is feasible is frequently deeply believed in by innovators and creators. Belief power plays a major role in the fields of advertising and persuasion. Persuasive strategies are used by marketers to develop a positive image and increase demand by attempting to shape consumer beliefs about their products and services. Social movements and revolutionary movements have historically been propelled by shared convictions. Consensus about the need for change gave power to movements for women's suffrage, environmental protection, and civil rights. One important factor that shapes both our individual and communal experiences is the dynamic and multidimensional force known as the power of belief. The human state is fundamentally shaped by belief, which affects our ideas, emotions, and behaviors. To effectively use belief for personal development and constructive social change, we must first acknowledge its potential and how it can both empower and constrain us.

Clarity in Financial Goal Setting: Setting SMART (specific, measurable, achievable, relevant, and time-bound) financial objectives is something we highly emphasize. Set specific goals for your financial path to give it emphasis and direction. Effective financial management for your personal or business needs starts with setting clear financial goals. Your financial journey will be facilitated by these goals, which give you a road map for setting priorities, making plans, and achieving your desired results. The significance and advantages of establishing specific financial goals are explained here. It offers direction and purpose for your financial decisions. Important questions like what you want to accomplish, when you want to accomplish it, and why it's necessary are all addressed by them. Your motivation and attention span are maintained by this clarity. Well-defined financial goals can be quite inspiring. You're more likely to stick with something and make the required decisions and sacrifices when you have clear objectives to work toward. Financial discipline can be strongly influenced by your desire to achieve your goals. Setting financial objectives enables you to prioritize your savings and expenditures. Allocating your resources (revenue) in a way that supports your objectives can be achieved by determining what matters most to you. This might help you avoid impulsive purchases and make sure that your money is going toward the things that are most important to you. Having specific goals gives you a way to gauge your success. You may monitor your financial progress to see if any changes are needed or if you are getting closer to your objectives. You may maintain accountability and make wise decisions by using this tracking procedure. Setting financial objectives is essential to developing a financial strategy and budget. Your objectives provide a framework for determining how much you should invest, save, or spend on various areas of your life. As a result, creating a budget that suits your needs is easier to manage. Financial objectives aid in risk management as well. You may evaluate the risks involved in accomplishing your goals and put plans in place to reduce them if you have well-defined objectives. This covers things like emergency savings, insurance, and a variety of investment options. Achieving long-term financial security requires having well-defined financial goals. Setting clear financial objectives will help you make sure you are ready for whatever comes next, be it home ownership, retirement savings, or paying for your kids' college tuition. Establishing financial objectives gives you the ability to steer your financial course. It causes you to think more strategically about financial decisions than reactively. More financial well-being and wiser financial decisions may result from this sense of empowerment. Setting and maintaining clear financial objectives is crucial, but it's also critical to be flexible. Your objectives may need to be modified as your circumstances change throughout life. Setting goals and then having the freedom to adjust them as needed are equally crucial. A sense of contentment and satisfaction can come from reaching your financial goals. It could give you more self-assurance in your financial skills and a feeling of achievement. Recognizing and appreciating your progress can be emotionally fulfilling and inspirational. One of the most important parts of financial planning and management is creating specific financial goals. It gives your financial decisions direction, meaning, and drive, assisting you in making wise judgments, maintaining accountability, and achieving financial success. Your financial path can be greatly aided by having clear and concise goals that you can work toward.

Adopting a Growth Mentality: In this section, we present the concept of a growth mindset, which is the conviction that your skills and intelligence can be enhanced by commitment and diligence. This way of thinking is crucial for overcoming obstacles and adjusting to shifting financial conditions. It entails taking up a particular set of attitudes and beliefs about learning and personal growth. It is the belief that with commitment, hard work, and the appropriate techniques, people can enhance and grow in their aptitudes, intelligence, and skills. This explains what it means to adopt a growth mindset and its advantages. Beginning with the core conviction that your skills and intelligence are not fixed attributes but rather may be improved over time, a growth mindset is established. A "fixed mindset," in which individuals feel their traits and skills are innate and unalterable, is in opposition to this viewpoint. Growth-minded people view difficulties, failures, and barriers as chances for improvement. Rather than shying away from challenging assignments, they welcome them, understanding that failure and struggle are essential components of learning. Adopting a development mindset means prioritizing perseverance and effort over natural aptitude or intelligence. This kind of person knows that the secret to growth and achievement is to work hard and remain committed to one's objectives.

Positive criticism and comments are seen as important sources of knowledge for personal development. Those who have a growth mentality utilize criticism as an opportunity to improve their abilities and capabilities rather than taking it personally. Individuals possessing a growth mentality derive inspiration from the accomplishments of others rather than feeling intimidated or jealous of their success. They view accomplishments as proof that, with the correct strategy and work, advancement and growth are achievable. A growth mentality is flexible and receptive to new ideas. It acknowledges that situations, information, and abilities change and that people need to constantly learn and adapt to succeed. Instead of running from obstacles, those who have a growth mentality actively seek them out. They know that pushing themselves beyond their comfort zones helps them develop and stretch their skills. Adopting a growth attitude promotes resilience when faced with obstacles. People who have this mentality are more inclined to pick themselves up after failing, grow from their errors, and keep pursuing their objectives. Individuals with a development mentality typically do better in school, at work, and in their personal lives, according to research. They work harder and use more productive learning techniques because they think they can get better, which can boost their self-worth, lower their stress levels, and improve their general well-being. It enables people to take on obstacles with optimism and positivity, which can result in a more contented existence. Adopting a belief system that promotes growth, resilience, and a love of learning is what it means to embrace a growth mindset. Encouragement to view obstacles and setbacks as chances rather than threats can ultimately result in higher levels of motivation, improved output, and greater contentment in both one's personal and professional lives. People with a growth mindset can continuously pursue excellence and realize their full potential because they recognize that they are in control of their growth and improvement.

The Function of Patience and Persistence: We talk about how crucial patience and persistence are to accumulating wealth. Often, achieving financial success takes time; therefore, it's important to stick with your plans even in the face of obstacles. To succeed and accomplish one's objectives in a variety of spheres of life, two fundamental traits are required: patience and persistence. They support people in overcoming obstacles on the path to long-term success and are frequently referred to as the "twin pillars of progress." This explains the functions of perseverance and patience. Patience is the capacity to maintain composure and calmness in the face of obstacles and setbacks. It makes it possible for people to tackle problems calmly and logically, as opposed to getting angry or depressed. Being patient helps people concentrate on long-term objectives and results. That helps individuals realize that big things rarely happen quickly and that shortcuts and quick fixes are rarely the way to long-term success. It is essential to the decision-making process. It enables people to avoid making snap decisions by allowing them to thoroughly consider their options, obtain pertinent information, and make educated judgments. Developing and sustaining healthy partnerships requires patience. It entails listening, comprehending, and allowing people the space and time necessary for self-expression and personal development. Patience cultivates empathy and collaboration in both personal and professional interactions. These people are tolerant of ambiguity and uncertainty. Persistence is the will and fortitude to get over challenges and disappointments in a world that is frequently unpredictable. People who can wait for the appropriate opportunity and adjust to changing conditions are more likely to succeed. It entails persevering through challenges and keeping up your efforts to achieve your objectives, even when things get hard. Continuous practice and improvement are necessary for many abilities and successes. Whether learning to play an instrument, play a sport, or acquire a professional skill, persistence is essential to success in any endeavor. It's persistence that makes dreams come true. It is the act of continuously moving forward with your goals, despite obstacles or lead times. Goals are just dreams if they are not pursued. This calls for flexibility and the readiness to change course when called upon. It is figuring out different ways to get to the same place rather than obstinately following a failing line of action. People who persevere are more likely to overcome obstacles and disappointments. They keep going after making the required corrections, learning from their mistakes, and eventually advancing, which ultimately promotes both professional and personal progress. A culture of ongoing learning and development is fostered by persistence. It motivates people to push themselves and look for ways to get better, which results in increased personal growth and skill sets. The complementing traits of perseverance and patience enable people to overcome obstacles in life and make progress toward their objectives. While persistence feeds the will to overcome setbacks and carry on pursuing one's goals, patience offers the required serenity and long-term perspective. They work well together to provide a potent mixture that can promote achievement and personal development in a variety of spheres of life.

The book's opening highlights the fact that wealth creation and preservation include more than just sound financial planning and investing methods. A holistic approach to wealth management and the development of the proper mindset are equally important. The book's structure and inspiration for readers to start their financial success path are based on the extraordinary millionaire mindset.

CHAPTER 1: DISCOVERING PURPOSE

A Moment Of Clarity

When a person realizes their life's purpose or mission, is described in This revelation, discovery, or gradual awakening that gives them insight into what matters most and what they intend to do with their lives might be called a moment of clarity. It entails investigating one's beliefs, interests, passions, and skills to find purpose and direction. Time, introspection, and self-reflection may be required for this process. A sudden and unexpected realization can occasionally lead to a "lightbulb moment." It can feel like a flash of insight and can happen during a particular event, at a crisis point, or through a random encounter. Gaining a deeper understanding of one's values, beliefs, emotions, motivations, strengths, weaknesses, and personal identity is the process of self-discovery. To find one's true nature and essence requires introspection, reflection, and exploration. The process of self-discovery is a lifetime endeavor that is essential to one's development as a person, their self-awareness, and their authenticity. Examining one's thoughts, feelings, and inner experiences is called introspection, and it usually starts there. It entails examining one's inner world to obtain understanding and posing questions such as "Who am I?" and "What do I value?" Gaining insight into your fundamental values and beliefs—which form the basis for your actions and decisions—is a necessary step towards self-discovery. Making decisions in life can be guided by determining what matters most to you. A vital component of self-discovery is developing emotional awareness. It entails being aware of and cognizant of your emotions, as well as knowing how to control them and how they affect your behavior. Finding your drives, passions, and interests is a key component of self-discovery. It's about realizing your motivations and the things in life that make you happy and fulfilled. Recognizing your advantages and disadvantages is another aspect of self-discovery. Understanding your areas of strength and potential for improvement will help you grow both personally and professionally. Self-discovery is mostly dependent on your life experiences, both good and bad. Your viewpoint, convictions, and sense of self are shaped by them. You can gain a better understanding of yourself by reflecting on these situations. You can clarify and enhance your sense of self through self-discovery. It's about finding an answer to the question, "Who am I?" and creating a self-concept that aligns with your principles and convictions. Authenticity is promoted through the self-discovery process. Living by your values, beliefs, and self-identity entails staying loyal to who you are. This is a tool for development and betterment on a personal level. Once you are aware of your advantages and disadvantages, you may focus on developing your strong points and improving your weak points. Self-discovery can provide you with new perspectives that inform decisions about your relationships, profession, and personal objectives, among other areas of your life. A more purposeful and meaningful existence may result from it.

Self-discovery is a voyage of introspection that lasts a lifetime and enables people to understand themselves, their values, beliefs, emotions, and motives better. It is an effective instrument for developing oneself, leading a genuine life, and creating deep connections. The development of self-awareness via self-discovery is essential to human growth and welfare. Finding one's purpose usually coincides with one's basic principles. It has the same feeling as discovering a purpose or calling in life that truly aligns with one's values and beliefs. A flash of insight gives one a fresh perspective and sense of direction. A significant shift in priorities may result from it, enabling people to focus their energies on the things that are most important to them. Motivation spikes are frequently experienced after discovering one's mission. People discover a newfound motivation and drive to work toward their goals when they understand why they are doing what they are doing. People may have profound life changes as a result of this pivotal occasion. It could lead to changes in their personal relationships, careers, or way of life to better fit their newfound purpose. A strong sense of contentment and life satisfaction are frequently brought about by living in harmony with one's mission. The objectives and actions are no longer viewed as obligations but rather as chances to further a greater good. Many people who realize their purpose in life go on to positively influence society, their town, or the entire world. They frequently have greater motivation to contribute and create a lasting impression. It signifies an alteration or impact that furthers the welfare of people, groups, institutions, or the general public. Positive influence can take many different forms, but what makes it important is that it has the power to bring about changes that are both desired and significant. Aiming to address societal issues and advance social good, positive impact initiatives include charitable endeavors, social projects, and community development programs. Vulnerable or underprivileged groups may profit from these initiatives. Environmentally beneficial initiatives include those that lessen pollution, preserve resources, or advance sustainable lifestyles. For both present and future generations, this results in a wealthier Earth. Positive corporate outcomes can stimulate the economy and create jobs. At the local, national, and international levels, innovation, entrepreneurship, and investments can propel economic development. Positive effects from technological breakthroughs are frequently seen in the enhancement of communication, convenience, and efficiency. They can improve our daily lives and revolutionize industries. Innovation and creativity that have a positive influence generate new ideas, solutions, and artistic expressions that improve our lives and advance society. Positive impact encompasses a wide range of actions and initiatives that create desirable, constructive, and beneficial outcomes. On a personal level, positive impact can be experienced through self-improvement efforts such as acquiring new skills, fostering meaningful relationships, or adopting healthy habits. It is essential to societal improvement, personal development, communal expansion, and the health of both people and the environment. A better, more sustainable, and peaceful world results from the efforts of individuals, organizations, and society to have a positive impact. A eureka moment is not always a static epiphany. Over time, as new experiences and insights impact a person's path, their understanding of their purpose may change. Refinement and expansion are continuous processes. It can give one's life purpose, direction, and inspiration. It is a potent and intensely personal experience. It's a time when people realize what matters to them and why they are here, and it can have a positive impact on both the individual and society. A crucial aspect of human development is the process of self-discovery.

Be Slow and Steady To Win the Race

This age-old proverb, which is frequently ascribed to "The Tortoise and the Hare," captures a valuable lesson about perseverance and attainment. The tortoise in the narrative eventually prevailed because of its unchanging resolve and persistence, despite the hare's skill and speed. This message, which emphasizes the value of consistent development and persistence in the pursuit of one's objectives and dreams, is straightforward but profound, making it a cornerstone of motivation.

In today's fast-paced environment, it's easy to fall in love with shortcuts, quick wins, and instant satisfaction. That being said, the wisdom of "be slow and steady" promotes an alternative strategy that is based on perseverance, consistency, and a long-term outlook. Let's explore how this phrase might be used as an effective means of inspiration. Many times, success calls for patience. It's about realizing that permanent success is not always reflected in short-term outcomes and that significant accomplishments require time. Choosing patience as a virtue can be an inspiration in a society where everything moves quickly and in a hurry. You may maintain your motivation through difficult times by realizing that slow development is a sign of dedication rather than a sign of failure. To become an expert at anything or accomplish any goal, you must be consistent. Instead of running, the tortoise advanced gradually, step by step. A key component of success is this constancy. You gradually gain momentum when you commit to persistent work, even on days when you lack enthusiasm.

It can be encouraging to know that your consistent improvement builds up and compounds. Setting realistic, attainable goals is crucial to winning the race. Excessive ambition or rash goal-seeking can cause dissatisfaction and burnout. When you observe small steps toward your bigger goals and establish attainable goals, motivation flourishes. There will inevitably be setbacks and challenges in life. The Turtle didn't let the horse's initial lead distract it from the ultimate aim. This persistence might act as a source of motivation when you meet hardships. By perceiving barriers as chances for growth and learning, you can keep your determination and focus on the finish line. On the path towards your goals, it's crucial to appreciate tiny triumphs along the way. These moments of appreciation provide a motivating boost and strengthen your dedication. Every stride forward, no matter how slow, is a step closer to your target. The tortoise's approach supports personal growth and development. It's not just about reaching the finish line; it's also about maturing as an individual throughout the road. The drive to become a better version of oneself may be a tremendous motivating force. Being slow and steady cultivates resilience; it helps you see clearly. When you embrace this mindset, you build the power to bounce back from failures and setbacks. Resilience is an important factor in motivation because it helps you persist in the face of adversity.

Long-Term Success:

Success is not about winning one race; it's about keeping a track record of accomplishments over the long haul. By adopting the "be slow and steady" approach, you prepare yourself for continuous success. This picture of long-term achievement can be immensely inspiring. The age-old wisdom of "be slow and steady" acts as a motivational attitude that reminds us of the value of patience, persistence, and determination in the pursuit of our goals. It encourages us to focus on the process, not just the outcome, and to regard every step forward as a win. With this perspective, motivation becomes a consistent companion on our journey toward permanent achievement, personal improvement, and a more rewarding life. Long-term success refers to consistent and permanent achievements, accomplishments, and affluence that are neither short-lived nor ephemeral. It shows a constant track record of positive outcomes, growth, and success in various facets of life, whether it's personal, professional, or organizational. Long-term success is marked by its ability to resist obstacles, setbacks, and the test of time. It is marked by its capacity to be maintained over a lengthy period of time. It is not dependent on fast fixes, shortcuts, or fleeting trends. Instead, it focuses on practices and policies that are environmentally, socially, and economically sustainable. Long-term success is characterized by a pattern of consistent achievements. It is not about isolated, infrequent wins but rather about maintaining a favorable trajectory over a sustained period. To achieve long-term success, individuals, organizations, or systems need to be resilient. They must bounce back from adversities, adjust to changing conditions, and continue to make progress despite setbacks.

Long-term success is related to the creation of enduring value. This value can emerge in different ways, including financial stability, brand reputation, personal growth, or social effect. The benefits provided by long-term success continue to accrue over time. Achieving this typically requires needs rigorous strategic planning. It entails setting clear objectives, developing a roadmap for reaching those objectives way, and making thoughtful and informed decisions along the route. Success hinges on a commitment to constant learning and change. Individuals or organizations must stay up-to-date with emerging trends, technology, and best practices to remain competitive and relevant. While pursuing long-term success, risk management is vital. It entails identifying potential risks and executing procedures to mitigate them, ensuring that unanticipated problems do not derail the journey. Building and maintaining great connections with stakeholders, whether they are customers, partners, or workers, is a vital aspect of long-term success. These relationships can contribute to loyalty and support over time. Conducting company or personal pursuits with ethics and principles at the forefront is a characteristic of long-term success. Such behaviors establish trust, trustworthiness, and a positive reputation that may be perpetuated over time. Long-term success frequently involves creativity and adaptability. This involves being open to change, investigating new opportunities, and always seeking ways to develop and adapt. Monitoring, measuring, and assessing progress is vital for long-term success. It enables modifications and enhancements along the way, ensuring that goals are being reached and strategies stay effective. Long-term success goes beyond personal or immediate advantages. It is typically related to the desire to leave a legacy, create a lasting impression, and contribute to the advancement of society or the world at large. In personal terms, long-term success entails continual personal progress and enjoyment. It is striving for a life that is meaningful, satisfying, and aligned with one's values and objectives. This signifies the ability to produce enduring and sustained progress, growth, and success in various spheres of life. It is not just about short-lived triumphs but about permanent value, perseverance, and a commitment to continual progress. Achieving long-term success needs careful planning, adaptability, ethical standards, and a focus on producing a positive and lasting influence.

CHAPTER 2: FAILURE IS A CHOICE:

Never Let Bad Situations Get The Best Of You

This slogan expresses a powerful perspective on dealing with hardships and disappointments in life. It reminds us that we have the ability to choose how we respond to hard circumstances, and it develops an attitude of resilience and determination. Understanding Failure as a Choice At first glance, the notion that failure is a decision may seem illogical. After all, no one consciously seeks failure, and it often comes unexpectedly. However, the remark doesn't mean that we consciously choose to fail but rather that our attitude toward failure is a choice. It highlights our ability to choose how we interpret and react to setbacks. Life is filled with ups and downs, and adversity is an inherent part of the human experience. Whether it's personal, professional, or societal issues, awful events are sure to happen. The important thing is how we respond to these problems. By choosing resilience, we may bounce back from failures, learn from our experiences, and develop stronger in the process. Failure, rather than being a dead end, can serve as a valuable teacher. When we confront hardship, we have a choice: we may let it defeat us, or we can learn from it. Failure provides insights into what went wrong, what can be improved, and how to make better choices in the future. It's an opportunity for growth and self-improvement. Choosing not to allow unfavorable situations to get the best of us means having a positive mindset and viewpoint. It entails seeking silver linings, recognizing possibilities inside problems, and having a cheerful view. This perspective helps us to navigate adversity with grace and persistence. The statement underlines personal accountability. It argues that we have control over our reactions and attitudes when presented with bad events. By taking control of our responses, we become active players in our own lives rather than passive victims of events. Choosing not to surrender to terrible conditions demands perseverance and determination. It means continuing through problems, retaining concentration on our goals, and refusing to be distracted by transitory setbacks. This steadfast devotion is frequently the driving force behind final achievements. Instead of viewing terrible events as insurmountable obstacles, we might choose to perceive them as chances for growth and transformation. Each setback can be a stepping stone toward our goals, delivering significant lessons and experiences that help us improve as people. Emotional resilience is the ability to adapt and bounce back from hardship. Choosing not to allow terrible situations to get the best of us includes establishing emotional resilience. This comprises coping skills, stress management tactics, and the ability to keep cool under duress. This perspective can be a source of inspiration and motivation. It reminds us that we are not powerless in the face of hardships and disappointments. We have the potential to rise above hardship, emerge stronger, and continue advancing toward our ambitions.

While we have the capacity to select our attitude to adversity, it's crucial to understand the role of community and support. Seeking aid, guidance, and encouragement from others can be crucial in our capacity to overcome challenging situations.

Always remember Failure is a decision. When life knocks you down you can choose whether to get back up. Underscores the value of personal agency and resilience in the face of hardship. It emphasizes that while we may not control all circumstances of our lives, we do have power over our responses and attitudes. By choosing resilience, learning from setbacks, and maintaining a positive perspective, we may overcome adversity and continue to pursue our goals and aspirations with unflinching resolve. This attitude helps us to tackle life's uncertainties with courage and grace, ultimately leading to personal growth and long-term success.

Building Wealth By Creating Your Own Path

Building wealth is a goal that many individuals desire to achieve, as it offers financial security, freedom, and the capacity to pursue one's dreams and goals. However, the path to riches is not one-size-fits-all, and there are various paths to establishing financial prosperity. "Creating your own path" in wealth building says that individuals have the power to design their unique journey and tactics for gaining money. It highlights the significance of individualized, inventive, and adaptive strategies to attain financial success. Creating your own road to wealth is an empowering and dynamic experience. It acknowledges that wealth building is a highly customized process that involves a combination of financial knowledge, strategy, adaptability, and tenacity. By defining your unique vision, personalizing your strategies, and remaining committed to continuous learning and adaptability, you can navigate the complexities of wealth building and work towards achieving your financial goals, ultimately securing your financial future and enjoying the benefits that wealth can bring.

3 Key Principles for Building Wealth

One of the core foundations for constructing your own road to prosperity is obtaining financial literacy. Understanding principles like budgeting, investing, debt management, and taxation is vital. This knowledge helps individuals to make informed decisions regarding their money.

• **Setting Clear Goals:** Defining defined and measurable financial goals is key. Whether it's saving for retirement, acquiring a home, establishing a business, or any other ambition, having clear goals provides direction and drive for wealth growth. Building wealth frequently begins with efficient planning and saving. By developing a budget that corresponds with your financial goals and saving frequently, you can ensure that you are continually putting money aside for future investments and possibilities. Investing plays a major role in financial development. Among other things, people can invest in stocks, bonds, real estate, and businesses. Making an investment strategy that works for your time horizon, financial goals, and risk tolerance is essential to success.

• **Debt Management:** Another crucial element of building wealth is minimizing and controlling debt. Developing a strategy to pay down debt and steer clear of unnecessary new loans is essential because high-interest loans, such as credit card debt, can hinder your financial success. Income increases are one of the primary drivers of wealth. Creating a side business, investing in education and skill development, creating passive income streams, or progressing in your work are some ways to do this. To increase wealth, financial risks must be assessed and managed. This means purchasing insurance, diversifying one's financial holdings, and preparing for unanticipated expenses or emergencies.

• **Describe Your Vision:** Once you have your unique path to wealth mapped out, tell us about it. For you, what does possessing money mean? What are your financial goals? Having a clear vision will make you more motivated and focused. Recognize that the best course of action for you may differ from that of someone else. Your objectives, level of risk tolerance, and financial situation are unique. Make sure your strategies are tailored to your particular circumstances. Maintain your commitment to lifelong learning. Since the financial landscape is constantly shifting, staying informed on the most recent opportunities and risks is essential. Continue your education in personal finance, wealth-building strategies, and investing. Be prepared to adjust your wealth-building strategies when circumstances change. Flexibility is crucial because goals, circumstances, and the economy can all change over time. When in doubt, seek advice from financial experts, including financial consultants, accountants, and estate planners. Their guidance can help you make educated decisions and navigate challenging financial issues. Building wealth requires discipline, time, and patience. When making financial decisions, avoid making rash choices and focus on the bigger picture. Consider how your unique skills and aptitudes can help you in your pursuit of financial success. Make the most of your distinctive traits for your creative endeavors, business ventures, and career. Cooperation and networking are usually helpful in gaining riches. Developing relationships with mentors, coworkers, and potential business partners can result in opportunities for knowledge sharing. Be open to new ideas and resources that can help you in your pursuit of wealth accumulation, as well as new approaches to managing your finances and researching potential investments.

CHAPTER 3: INTEREST AND PAYOUTS FROM PASSIVE INCOME SOURCES

It is possible to make passive revenue with little or no ongoing labor. It usually has to do with money and investments that yield returns whether or not you work a job. Interest and dividends are two common sources of passive income. In this talk, we will look at several income streams, their characteristics, and how they could be useful components of a diversified investment portfolio. Interest and dividends are significant passive income sources that present opportunities for wealth accumulation, flexibility, and stability. Investing in stocks, bonds, or dividend-paying, interest-bearing financial instruments allows individuals to build a diversified portfolio that produces steady, predictable income. These revenue streams, which are essential components of a comprehensive financial strategy, can help you achieve your short- and long-term financial goals. Dividends are payments provided by corporations to their shareholders; they are often derived from earnings. As a portion of the company's earnings, they are distributed to shareholders. company's stock. To be eligible for dividends, a company's stock must be owned in shares. Companies may pay out dividends to investors from their profits. One of the key advantages of dividends is that they provide a reliable stream of income. Because well-established companies usually pay dividends regularly, they are a dependable source of passive income. The amount of money you get in dividends is known as your dividend yield. It is calculated by deducting the current market price of the stock from the annual dividend amount. This percentage might help you assess the potential return on your investment. Dividends can be a useful component of a diversified investing strategy. Investing in stocks from multiple companies and industries lets you spread your risk while still earning dividends. Some companies increase their dividend payments over time, which could lead to a rise in passive income. Purchasing dividend-growth companies could be an intelligent choice if you want to capitalize on this possibility. Dividends are a tax-effective passive income source because they may be taxed less heavily in some jurisdictions than other forms of income.

Interest revenue is produced by making loans to individuals or businesses in exchange for regular interest payments. There are numerous ways to generate this form of passive income, which is accessible through various financial instruments. Potential sources of interest income include bonds, certificates of deposit (CDs), savings accounts, and peer-to-peer lending platforms. When you invest or make deposits in these options, interest is paid to you over time. The amount of money you can earn depends on the type of investment and level of risk involved. For example, corporate bonds may give higher returns than savings accounts, which usually have lower interest rates. The liquidity of various interest-bearing investments varies. While some may let you access your money more quickly than others, some may have lengthier maturity periods. Compound interest is a useful tactic for growing your passive income. It means that interest will be earned on both the principal and the interest that has already been accumulated. Over time, this compounding effect might significantly increase your wealth. Just like dividend income, interest income can also be a part of a diversified portfolio. Several interest-bearing investments can help you minimize your risk and generate a consistent stream of passive income. Interest payments are often consistent and predictable. Financial planning is made easier when you know in advance when and how much interest you will get. Passive income provides financial stability and a safety net because it can be used to supplement your main income or cover essential expenses. If you have a passive income, you can more freely and flexibly manage your time and lifestyle. It can free you from the constraints of a typical 9–5 job. Passive income is a very powerful tool for wealth creation and can help you raise your net worth over time. Many people rely on passive income sources like dividends and interest during their retirement years. When you're not working, it might provide a reliable source of income. Passive income sources can increase the diversification of your investment portfolio by reducing risk and volatility. Some passive income sources provide tax benefits, so you might be able to keep more of your profits.

Bequests and Original Works

Royalties and intellectual property are connected concepts that are significant when it comes to creative and inventive endeavors. They deal with providing protection and remuneration to original inventors and owners of intellectual property, which include inventions, artistic creations, and other forms of creative expression. We'll go into great detail about intellectual property and royalties, including what they are, how they work, and how crucial they are to certain businesses. Royalties and intellectual property are necessary to safeguard and reward writers and innovators. They promote cultural diversity, boost economic expansion, and offer rewards for ingenuity. Intellectual property rights and royalty regimes, despite their complexity and multifaceted nature, are indispensable for promoting innovation and defending the rights of creators and innovators across various industries and fields.

Royalties are sums of money paid to the owner or creator of intellectual property in exchange for its use, exploitation, or licensing. These payments are typically calculated as a percentage of sales or earnings from the intellectual property. Royalties usually occur when the owner of intellectual property grants permission for someone else to use it. For example, an artist may agree to pay a film producer royalties for using their song in the film in exchange for receiving payment for each copy that is purchased or viewed. The specific terms of royalties are typically outlined in a license or contract agreement. Among the factors that could be used to calculate royalties are a set fee per use, usage, or sale. There might be large variations in the percentage of revenue or profit allotted to royalties for the owner. How long royalties are paid for is determined by the terms of the agreement. It can be paid in full upfront, in installments over a set period, or in the form of royalties for the term that the intellectual property is protected. It protects the rights and interests of people who produce and own intellectual property. They make sure that these individuals or groups are compensated for the effort and creativity they put forth.

Intellectual Property (IP): Names, symbols, artwork, inventions, literary works, and photographs exploited for commercial purposes are all regarded as works of the mind. It's a kind of intangible property that is legally protected and grants owners and artists the sole right to their creations. The primary classifications of intellectual property are as follows:

Copyright protects original literary and artistic works, including music, paintings, and novels.

For a predetermined period, inventors can control how and when their innovations are used and commercialized by using patents.

Domain Names: Trademarks are distinctive signs, logos, or symbols used in the marketplace to distinguish one product or service from another.

Trade secrets are confidential business information that provides a business with a competitive advantage. Formulas, customer lists, and production techniques are a few examples.

"Industrial design" is the preservation of an object's general shape or surface ornamentation.

Intellectual property and royalties are significant.

Royalties and other types of intellectual property encourage innovation by providing producers and innovators with the motivation to create new works. When people are certain that their creative endeavors will yield financial rewards, it encourages them to keep going.

One way intellectual property owners can profit from their works is through royalties. They can sustain their standard of living and make further investments in new projects because of the income their intellectual property generates. Works cannot be copied or used without permission, thanks to intellectual property rights protection. People and corporations are motivated to respect the rights of creators and secure proper licensing because of the possibility of legal action as well as financial gain.

Financial Progress Royalties and intellectual property are significant forces behind economic expansion. They assist sectors including technology, entertainment, and pharmaceuticals, promote innovation, and promote economic growth and employment creation.

Foreign Currency: There are significant implications in the domains of intellectual property and royalties. Fair competition is promoted by ensuring that innovators and inventors from one nation are protected and paid for their work when they are used in other nations.

Variety in Visual Arts and Culture: By preserving and expanding a wide range of artistic expressions, intellectual property rights, and royalties, we foster variety in culture and the arts. This contributes to the global preservation of languages, civilizations, and artistic manifestations.

Consumers' Trust: When consumers have access to genuine, superior products and services, they stand to gain from intellectual property rights and royalties. These rights aid in ensuring that goods are authentic and match specifications.

Boosting and generating passive revenue:

The creation of passive income is one financial tactic that can result in long-term flexibility, financial security, and financial independence. Passive income is a good source of income if you want to diversify your sources and lessen your reliance on regular labor because it takes little to no active effort or commitment. This in-depth discussion will cover the idea of generating and increasing passive income, the range of workable approaches, and the actions necessary to reach this financial objective. One strategy for achieving long-term stability and financial independence is to develop and grow passive income. You can attain your financial goals and experience financial freedom by creating many passive income sources and continuously reinvesting, diversifying, and increasing your endeavors. To be able to make wise financial decisions, the important thing is to start early, stick with it, and never stop learning. Real estate, internet companies, investing, and other passive income sources are all excellent choices. Passive income is produced by investing in or using procedures that yield consistent income with little ongoing work. Investing is one of the most commonly used methods for obtaining passive income. This holds for properties, stocks, bonds, and real estate that generate dividends. Dividends, capital gains, or monthly interest payments may eventually be received from these investments. One can own and rent out real estate, such as homes or businesses, as a stable source of passive income. Rent can cover expenses and turn a profit. If you purchase dividend-paying stocks, you are entitled to a regular dividend payment from the company's profits. These payouts can indicate a steady stream of revenue.

You can lend money to people or small businesses through platforms like Lending Club and Prosper in return for interest payments. You can both help people receive funding and earn passive income by employing this method. As a creative or innovator, royalties and licensing sales from your intellectual property—such as books, music, or patents—can generate passive income for you. A successful blog or YouTube channel can lead to passive income streams from advertising, sponsorships, and affiliate marketing. Content development can eventually pay off, even with the initial outlay of funds. To progressively amass riches without having to work for it, you can set up automatic savings and investment plans. Over time, the value of regular contributions made to investment or retirement accounts may increase.

Once you establish a passive income stream, the idea is to grow it gradually to achieve your objectives and improve your financial stability. Consider investing a portion of your passive income back into your income-producing investments rather than consuming the entire amount. In the long run, this might quicken growth. You can lower your risk and possibly raise your passive income by spreading your investments over several asset classes and businesses. Stability and growth potential can be obtained by combining bonds, equities, and real estate. Continue producing fresh material or making consistent investments to bring in passive income. To increase your income over time, you must remain consistent. Keep yourself updated and knowledgeable about the strategies you are employing to bring in passive income. Making wise judgments that lead to success can be facilitated by having a thorough understanding of the markets, trends, and possibilities. To generate passive revenue, come up with innovative ways to collaborate with others in your field or industry. Collaborations, joint ventures, and co-creation of content can help you reach a wider audience and even increase your revenue. Consider growing after you've determined which of your passive income strategies are effective. For instance, produce similar content to boost your earnings if a specific blog post or video brings in a sizable sum of money. To maximize your goals, seek advice from financial advisors or specialists in passive income. They can offer advice and insights pertinent to your financial objectives.

Opportunities for Side Income:

Financial security is provided by passive income, which also lessens the necessity for regular work. It provides the opportunity to follow one's interests and objectives. You can work whenever and wherever you choose if you have a passive income. Regardless of your choices, it can assist you in achieving a work-life balance. Passive income streams can help build wealth and long-term financial security over time. It lessens the risk of relying just on one source of income by enabling you to diversify them. Since the sources offer a steady stream of income after retirement, they are advantageous for retirement planning. By acting as a safety net against unforeseen bills or economic downturns, it can help lessen financial stress.

CHAPTER 4: OWNERSHIP OF BUSINESSES AND ENTREPRENEURS

Starting your own business can be an exciting and difficult undertaking, but it also offers the chance to transform your idea, skill, or passion into a lucrative effort and a source of personal fulfillment. For those who are prepared to invest the necessary time and energy, becoming an entrepreneur can prove to be a fulfilling career option, even with all of its risks and unknowns. Important decisions and steps to take while launching your own company.

Creative Concept Development and Market Analysis:

Every successful company begins with an idea. Determine your hobbies, abilities, and specializations first. Consider the difficulties or wants that your company can help with. To gain a better understanding of your target market, rivals, and industry trends, conduct an extensive market analysis. This first phase is essential for fine-tuning your concept and making sure there is a market for your product or service. Your project's road map is a carefully considered business plan. Included are a synopsis of your target market, sales and marketing plans, financial forecasts, operational specifics, and business objectives. A business plan is necessary to guide your company's growth, draw in investors, and obtain capital. Choose a reputable A limited liability company (LLC), corporation, partnership, or sole proprietorship are the possible organizational forms for your firm. Get your company registered with the appropriate government agencies and obtain the licenses and approvals that are required. Ascertain that you abide by local laws and tax regulations. The finest financing option for your company should be chosen. In addition to using your funds, you can seek investors, employ crowdsourcing, or submit an application for a small business loan. One way to make sure you have enough cash on hand to meet your company's needs is to properly monitor your budget. The infrastructure and location of your firm should be chosen. An actual store, a home office, a co-working space, or an e-commerce platform could be this, depending on your business idea. Take into consideration the tools, resources, and software you'll need.

To increase the awareness of your company, create a unique name, logo, and web presence. Describe in your marketing plan how to connect with and interact with your target market. Enhance brand exposure and draw in clients by utilizing online and offline marketing channels. Make the time to improve and enhance the products that your firm produces. Ensure they live up to the client's expectations as well as the quality requirements. Establish the procedures and policies required to continuously provide exceptional support if your company provides services. You might need to hire employees or contract workers as your business grows. Make intelligent choices about people who share the objectives and principles of your company. Assemble a capable group to help you accomplish your objectives. Keep accurate records of your finances and bookkeeping. It is possible to monitor income, expenses, and revenue with accounting software. To make well-informed decisions and guarantee the financial stability of your company, you must have a thorough financial management system. Establish strong bonds with your customers and put providing exceptional customer service first. Positive client experiences increase the likelihood that they will return and recommend your company to others. When your business grows, look for opportunities for growth and expansion. Take into account growing your customer base, offering a wider variety of goods and services, or breaking into untapped markets. Always have an adaptable plan in place in case the market or circumstances change. A key factor in the long-term success of your business will be your ability to innovate and move quickly. Obstacles and hazards are part of the entrepreneur lifestyle. Remain aware of any changes to laws or regulations that may affect your company. Ascertain that you abide by the rules about employment, taxes, and industry. Participate in business events, become a member of professional networks, and look for mentoring programs. By networking and pursuing ongoing education, you can give your company access to important knowledge and support. Think about your long-term goals for the company, as well as your plan of departure. A clear plan for the future is essential, regardless of your plans to sell the company, give it to a relative, or keep it open indefinitely. It takes perseverance, commitment, and meticulous planning to launch your firm, which is a major endeavor. Despite the risks, a strong chance exists for both financial and personal fulfillment. You may increase the likelihood that your business will be successful and last a long time by paying attention to this important advice and being strategic. Keeping this in mind will help your business grow and succeed because beginning a business is a journey.

Holding Shares in Different Companies

Holdings in other companies, or stocks, can be a profitable and prudent way to diversify your assets and build wealth. It comprises putting money into startups or established businesses to turn a profit on the shares or ownership stakes you purchase. Buying stocks, obtaining venture capital financing, or obtaining private equity are some of how one can engage in this type of investment. One clever way to build wealth and benefit from other people's successes in business is to invest in other companies. Opportunities for significant financial gain and possible income production are presented. It is not without risk, though, and it docs require some thought, diligence, and knowledge of your financial objectives and risk tolerance. Your odds of reaching your investing goals and long-term financial stability will be increased if you approach company investments with diligence and knowledge.

Purchasing stocks is one of the five categories of business investments. One of the most common ways to invest in business is through publicly traded firms. Investors can profit from dividend payments and capital growth by purchasing these shares, which are listed on stock exchanges.

The act of purchasing stock or other ownership holdings in privately held companies is known as private equity investment. Assuming managerial or decision-making responsibilities within the company may be one of these investments, which may require a large financial commitment.

Investments in early-stage or startup businesses with the potential for rapid growth are frequently financed using venture capital. Usually playing a leading role in the company's growth, venture capitalists provide money in exchange for stock.

In exchange for a stake in the business, angel investors provide money to start-ups or small enterprises. In addition to financial aid, they often provide experience, coaching, and networking opportunities.

Investing in real estate might involve purchasing either residential or commercial properties. Over time, real estate can increase in value and provide revenue from rentals.

There are two advantages to investing in other companies: portfolio diversification and risk distribution among various asset types. By keeping your portfolio diverse, you can lower your total risk of investing. Especially for startups or companies with great promise, investing in enterprises can yield enormous profits. Depending on the kind of investment you make, you may have the opportunity to become a part owner and influence the company's decisions and course. Corporate assets that yield consistent income streams in the form of dividends or rental payments include dividend-paying equities and rental properties.

Essential Things to Think about If Investing in Other Businesses: Exemptions from capital gains tax on long-term investments and real estate depreciation are two examples of tax incentives for business investments.

Ability to Adjust to Danger: Before making any business investments, ascertain your level of risk appetite. Different investment types carry varying degrees of risk, so it's critical to match your investments to your financial goals and risk tolerance.

Investigating and Taking Precautions: Examine the companies you are thinking about investing in with a keen eye. Consider their development potential, market conditions, management team, and financial situation. Choose the length of time you want to commit. What is your objective, accumulating money over time or short-term profits? Time horizon and investing strategy should coincide. Divide your money among a variety of sectors, industries, and asset classes. Both risk and the possibility of successful outcomes can be decreased using this approach. Take into account the amount you can and are willing to invest. Observe your financial situation. situation and refrain from taking on more than you can manage; make sure your getaway is well-planned. Prepare for a variety of exit scenarios by having a plan in place for when and how you wish to sell or liquidate your investments. Consult with professionals or financial advisors for advice on the best possible investing options and methods. Remain involved and closely monitor the success of your investments. Reaching your financial objectives requires routinely maintaining and modifying your investment portfolio.

Investing Techniques

Investment tactics are the plans and strategies people employ to use assets to reach their financial objectives. These concepts and methods include a broad spectrum of approaches that apply to real estate, equities, bonds, and other assets. Careful preparation and the use of strategies that fit your time horizon, risk tolerance, and financial goals are necessary for successful investment. We'll look at a variety of investing strategies in this talk and show you how to use them to make wise financial decisions.

1.   Purchase and Hold: The buy-and-hold strategy refers to investing in assets to hang onto them for a long period, usually decades or years. This strategy is predicated on the financial markets' historical rising trend. The goal of compound returns for investors is to increase the value of their investments over time. In general, buy-and-hold investors stick with their investments through market turbulence. The process of finding undervalued assets and purchasing them at a discount to their true value is known as value investing. This strategy's proponents hold that the market occasionally misprices assets, which presents chances for astute investors. Growth investors concentrate on companies that are anticipated to see large increases in sales and profitability, while value investors undertake in-depth research to find assets with solid fundamentals that are trading below their assessed fair value. When it comes

to assets with significant growth potential, investors using this technique are willing to pay more. Growth investors generally prefer businesses that finance innovation and expansion with their sales.

2. Momentum, Contrarian, and Dividend Investing: The main goal of dividend investing is to purchase assets that yield dividends regularly. Assets like dividend-paying stocks or real estate investment trusts (REITs), which provide owners a share of earnings, are typically preferred by investors looking for income streams. Finding a variety of assets, such as preferred stocks, bonds, and rental properties, that can provide income is the key to investing in income as opposed to dividends. Those who are looking for steady financial flow should use this strategy in particular. The fundamental idea behind momentum investing is that investments with a track record of high returns are likely to continue doing so shortly. Traders who want to profit from market sentiment and patterns use this strategy. Momentum investing is more risky and speculative since it entails purchasing assets

that have already increased in value. Going against the sentiment of the market is what it means to be a contrarian investor. Since discounted assets are not in the best interests of the majority of market participants, contrarian investors search for them. This strategy necessitates both a strong sense of conviction in one's opinion and the capacity to endure momentary market swings.

3. Control of Risk: An essential component of every investment plan is risk management. Investors evaluate their level of risk tolerance and put risk reduction plans into action. Common risk management strategies include diversifying your investments, using options and hedges, and setting up stop-loss orders. An essential element of effective investing is the use of investment methods. They assist investors in matching their investment plans to their time horizons, risk tolerance, and financial objectives. Before selecting an investment strategy, one should have a solid grasp of the assets under consideration. A well-balanced portfolio can use many strategies to achieve its goals and diversify

its risk. It is important to make well-informed judgments that align with your financial objectives and situation, whether you want to use fundamental or technical research, prioritize income, growth, or value, or adopt a buy-and-hold approach in the long run.

CHAPTER 5: PRESERVING WEALTH

The goal of wealth preservation as a financial strategy and way of thinking is to safeguard and preserve one's current assets and fortunes. It consists of a variety of procedures and methods intended to guarantee and safeguard the long-term viability of financial resources. This idea is particularly crucial for people and families that have amassed substantial wealth and want to preserve it for the next generations or to maintain their way of life throughout time. Tax optimization, estate planning, risk management, and asset allocation are a few more essential components of wealth preservation methods. People may make sure their wealth lasts by diversifying their portfolios, avoiding tax obligations, and practicing sensible investment management. This will allow them to support their loved ones through market and economic challenges and provide possibilities and financial stability. A comprehensive financial strategy must include wealth preservation, which can be customized to meet specific objectives like donating to charitable organizations, ensuring retirement comfort, or transferring wealth to future generations. To safeguard your money, you must carefully consider all of the risks that could deplete it, including inflation, market volatility, economic downturns, and unforeseen life occurrences. You may reduce the impact of these risks by utilizing risk management tools, diversifying your investments, and creating a well-thought-out financial strategy. One of the most important aspects of wealth preservation is appropriate asset allocation. It entails dividing your money among several asset classes, including cash, bonds, stocks, and real estate. By striving for steady, long-term development, this diversification helps shield your wealth from the ups and downs of specific markets. To protect wealth and make sure that assets are transferred to heirs and recipients smoothly, effective estate planning is essential. This covers creating trusts, appointing powers of attorney, and making wills. Lowering inheritance taxes and having control over how assets are allocated in line with your preferences are two other benefits of estate planning. Retirees need to learn how to manage their money if they want to keep living the way they do. Establishing a reasonable withdrawal plan, making sure you don't outlive your resources, and perhaps leaving an inheritance for your heirs are all examples of wealth preservation strategies. When it comes to wealth preservation, capital preservation typically takes precedence over rapid growth, which promotes a more conservative investment approach. This strategy seeks to shield your assets from large losses while reducing your exposure to market volatility. Due to the complexity of wealth preservation, a lot of people work with financial advisors, estate planners, and tax specialists to create and carry out their plans. These experts could provide wise advice and tailored solutions to protect your wealth. Maintaining wealth is a dynamic process that calls for flexibility and the capacity to modify plans in reaction to modifications in personal circumstances, tax regulations, and the financial environment. Proceeding Revised and updated wealth preservation plans must be evaluated and adjusted often. A thorough and progressive approach to wealth management is wealth preservation. It includes a variety of tactics meant to satisfy your financial objectives and needs while progressively safeguarding and increasing your assets. Wealth preservation is essential to making sure that your financial legacy lasts and helps you and your loved ones for many years to come, regardless of your goals—whether they are to finance your retirement, donate to charity, or leave something for your descendants.

Putting Money towards a Moral and Sustainable Family Legacy

Generating a family legacy through sustainable and ethical investing necessitates a conscientious, moral approach to wealth management. This approach combines a dedication to ethics, sustainability, and values with a track record of financial success. Creating a lasting and moral family legacy requires establishing a moral basis that directs financial decisions. The priorities, tenets, and beliefs of the family are embodied in these values. Among them include a dedication to social responsibility, environmental sustainability, and moral corporate conduct. Putting these ideals in writing ensures that all financial decisions are consistent with the family's values and acts as a compass. Selecting assets that satisfy predetermined criteria typically requires a laborious screening procedure when it comes to ethical and sustainable investing. Companies or sectors that engage in actions that are in opposition to the values of the family, including producing weapons, tobacco goods, or fossil fuels, might not be taken into account throughout this procedure. Positively, this may entail giving clean technology, renewable energy, and businesses with stellar social and environmental records priority when making investments. A long-term outlook is necessary when using ethical and sustainable investing to build a family legacy. This strategy aims for both short-term financial gain and long-term benefits. Long-term sustainable investment returns frequently surpass forecasts, demonstrating the financial advantages of upholding moral principles. Teaching and interacting with family members is essential to creating a family legacy. Talking about the family's moral investment ideas, beliefs, and intended impact on people of all ages is essential. A dedication to the family heritage and a common understanding is fostered by open and honest communication. Because ethical and sustainable investing can be complicated, it can be necessary to seek expert advice from financial advisors with experience in this area. These advisors may assist families with managing the complexities of ESG investing, evaluating the advantages of different investment options, and coordinating the portfolio with the family's long-term objectives. A fantastic approach to maintaining and developing your wealth, giving your family a lasting legacy, and improving society and the environment at the same time is to invest responsibly and ethically. This plan includes setting guiding principles, screening investments, including ESG factors, taking a long-term view, encouraging open communication within the family, and getting professional advice. Integrating sustainability and ethics into your investment strategy may enable you to leave a lasting legacy that upholds your family's principles and transforms the world for the better.

CHAPER 6: BEYOND EXPECTATIONS: ADJUSTING TO CHANGE

Two related ideas staying extraordinary and adapting to change discuss how people, companies, and organizations may embrace change and yet grow and surpass expectations. It is essential to embrace change as a chance for development and creativity in a world where change is a constant.

The only thing that is consistent in today's fast-paced world is change. Both individuals and organizations need to constantly adapt to changes in the economy, the consumer market, and technological improvements. Being exceptional requires understanding that change is a vital part of the modern world, not something to be disturbed. Change is not something to be dreaded or opposed; rather, it is an opportunity to innovate, advance, and outperform past successes. To stay exceptional, one must be dedicated to lifelong learning and development. This entails keeping an open mind, searching for fresh information, and honing the abilities required to prosper in changing environments. It also entails adopting a growth mindset, which sees obstacles as chances for advancement and creativity. Being receptive to fresh viewpoints and ideas will help you adjust to change more skillfully and produce exceptional outcomes.

Resilience and adaptability are characteristics of exceptional people and organizations. They adjust and withstand hardship without crumbling. Rather, they recover and discover new chances to succeed. Developing resilience entails learning how to bounce back from setbacks and adjust to unanticipated events. It means being adaptable, changing tactics, and coming up with creative solutions for problems as they come up. It frequently takes both inventiveness and imagination to stay remarkable. People and organizations need to foster an innovative culture to adjust to change efficiently. This entails motivating staff members to question the current quo, take chances, and be creative. Adaptability stems from creativity, which is also required to find novel solutions to problems. Planning is necessary to be outstanding more often than just reacting to change as it happens. Affluent individuals and institutions keep an eye on new trends and advancements in their sector or area of expertise. They are conscious of prospective obstacles and opportunities, therefore they take proactive measures to position themselves to benefit from changing circumstances. Successful change management frequently necessitates the creation of a strategic strategy. Good people and teams make detailed plans with clear goals and identify possible roadblocks and practical strategies for handling change. A road map for embracing opportunities and handling change without sacrificing quality is provided by strategic planning.

The capacity to react swiftly to change are traits of outstanding people and organizations. They can implement changes, shift course quickly, and make decisions without needless delay or red tape. Benefits like quickness and agility allow people and businesses to grow and adapt while holding onto their exceptional position in a world that is changing rapidly. Maintaining high standards necessitates building solid relationships and encouraging cooperation.

Through collaborations, information exchange, and mutual assistance, individuals and organizations can have access to the combined knowledge of disparate viewpoints. Cooperation can yield knowledge, assets, and solutions that boost flexibility. Maintaining a strong sense of purpose and clinging to fundamental beliefs are often necessary for being outstanding, even in the face of change. In turbulent times, this foundation offers direction and stability. It helps people and organizations stay true to their goals, identities, and basic principles in the face of changing tactics. Maintaining your exceptional needs constant introspection and assessment. It is essential to evaluate what is and is not functioning and to put the necessary changes into action. To stay ahead of the curve in a world that is constantly changing, one must be honest with oneself and commit to ongoing growth. Individuals and groups can develop the kind of thinking and matching behavior needed to continue being exceptional while adjusting to change. It entails being adaptable, persistent in learning, resilient, imaginative, proactive, foresighted, nimble, networking and laser-focused on one's basic principles. Together with goals in a world where things are changing all the time, developing these traits and habits will help you not only adapt to change successfully but also flourish and do incredible things. Maintaining exceptionality entails prospering in the face of change and going above and beyond expectations.

Ongoing Education and Personal Development

Since both professional and personal growth promotes a lifetime path of learning new skills, honing existing ones, and changing as people, they both call for continual education and self-improvement. This dedication to lifelong learning and growth is necessary for increasing one's personal and professional development as well as one's quality of life. We'll discuss the need for ongoing education and self-improvement in this in-depth discussion, along with offering practical guidance for taking this path. Professional growth and career advancement can result from a dedication to self-improvement. Gaining new abilities and keeping abreast of business advancements can increase output, create new opportunities, result in promotions, and raise pay. When people acquire new skills and information, their confidence frequently rises. This can lead to a more satisfied life and have a good effect on relationships in both the personal and professional spheres. Professional and personal development are both aspects of self-improvement. Developing interests, broadening one's perspectives, and learning new things all lead to a more fulfilling existence and higher levels of personal contentment. Continuous study improves one's problem-solving skills. It enables individuals to approach problems from several angles, draw from a variety of knowledge sources, and create original solutions. Creativity is enhanced in a state of self-actualization. It pushes people to think critically, take chances, and challenge the status quo. Combining knowledge from other fields leads to innovation, and continuing education makes this possible.

Effective Techniques for Ongoing Education and Personal Development:

Establish Specific Goals: Establish your goals for both your personal and academic growth first. Maintaining focus and motivation is facilitated by having a well-defined objective in sight. Create a thorough plan outlining your strategy for achieving your objectives. This could entail signing up for classes, going to seminars, reading books, or looking for mentors. Set aside a set amount of time each day or each month for self-improvement and learning. Maintaining consistency is essential for significant progress. Use educational apps, e-learning platforms, and online courses to access a wealth of knowledge. Education is now more accessible than ever before, all thanks to technology. Joining groups or professional organizations can provide access to useful resources, networking opportunities, and industry expertise. Seek input from teachers, mentors, or fellow students regularly to assess your development and pinpoint areas that require work. Adopt an inquiring mindset. Investigate new topics, ask questions, and keep an open mind to opposing viewpoints. Abundant curiosity is the motivating force behind lifelong learning. One of the best ways to increase your knowledge is to read. Examine a range of publications, including books, journals, and research papers, both related and unrelated to your field of study. Critical thinking includes problem-solving, reasoning, and information evaluation. Regularly engage in critical thinking exercises to improve your ability to make decisions. Take part in seminars, conferences, and workshops that are relevant to your field of interest. These gatherings offer chances for practical education and networking. Errors are excellent teaching moments. Recognize them, consider what went wrong, and use the insights to go forward. One of the best ways to support your learning is to teach. By imparting your knowledge to others, you deepen your understanding and accelerate your development.

Plan time to practice mindfulness and introspection. Think about your development trajectory, your advantages, and your places for improvement. Prioritizing career advancement over personal growth is crucial. During your leisure time, engage in activities and interests that enhance your general state of well-being. Both professional and personal development depend on ongoing education and self-improvement. They provide people with the tools they need to grow as individuals, progress in their careers, and deal with change. People can start a lifelong journey of development and improvement by embracing technology and a variety of learning tools, defining clear objectives, making a learning plan, and scheduling time for learning. Further crucial tactics for optimizing lifelong learning and personal development include maintaining curiosity, exercising critical thinking, asking for and accepting criticism, and accepting failure.

Sustaining Welfare and Income

The dynamic and intricate process of pursuing financial well-being while preserving one's physical, emotional, and mental health is known as "wealth and well-being balance." In a society where the never-ending quest for wealth can occasionally come at the expense of one's general well-being, striking this balance is essential. We will discuss the need to strike a balance between prosperity and well-being, possible issues, and workable solutions to reconcile these two fundamental components of life in this in-depth discussion.

Mental, physical, and emotional well-being are all included in the concept of well-being. Prioritizing acquiring wealth over other facets of life can result in tension, fatigue, and a lower quality of life. You can live a happy and fulfilling life by keeping a good balance between riches and well-being. Sustainability is encouraged by finding a balance between prosperity and well-being. In the end, going overboard in the chase of wealth can result in exhaustion, unhealthy lives, and damaged relationships. People can preserve their well-being and have a good impact on long-term performance by adopting a balanced approach. Relationships in the personal and professional spheres may suffer when money is the primary concern. Neglecting one's well-being can result in loneliness and the breakup of friendships, family ties, and professional relationships. Striking a balance between wealth and well-being fosters more positive interactions and better social ties. The capacity to overcome adversity and overall well-being are closely related. By emphasizing their well-being, people can become more emotionally and mentally resilient, which will enable them to face challenges head-on and with greater bravery and persistence.

Complexities Money and Well-Being in Balance: Prioritizing one's well-being can be difficult when there is a major distortion of personal and professional lives due to employment and career pressures. Occasionally, achieving financial achievement and fulfilling financial commitments trump the value of contentment and wellness. Because of the pressure that societal norms and expectations impose on these things, people may prioritize performance and financial prosperity over their well-being.

Realistic Methods for Juggling Money and Well-Being:

Establish priorities for your personal and professional life. What in life do you value most? This knowledge will direct your actions and assist you in striking a balance between prosperity and well-being. Establish distinct boundaries between your personal and professional lives. Set aside specified times for your family, work, and personal care. Respect these limits to maintain order. health practices that A healthy diet, regular exercise, meditation, and relaxation methods can all contribute to maintaining well-being. Although having wealth is vital, managing your money well is even more crucial. Refrain from accruing extra debt or making purchases that could be detrimental to your health. Establish tight bonds with your loved ones, friends, and colleagues. Emotional support from these relationships enhances well-being. Rather than segregating life and work, aim for harmony. A more harmonious merging of work and personal life is possible with this approach. Invest in self-improvement and continuing education to foster both professional and personal advancement. Financial success and well-being are associated with the growth of knowledge and skills. Acquire useful stress-reduction techniques, such as mindfulness and time management, to manage the pressure of building money. Make sure you are maintaining a healthy balance between wealth and well-being by taking regular stock of your life. As necessary, revise your actions and priorities. Never be afraid to ask for assistance when you need it or to assign duties and obligations to others. Maintaining well-being and reducing stress can be facilitated by relying on experts or support networks. Respect and acknowledge your accomplishments, whether they have to do with money or personal development. This encouraging reply may inspire you to keep looking for a balanced life. To be completely present and engaged in your daily activities, practice mindfulness. When you practice mindfulness, you can experience less anxiety and an increase in well-being. Achieving financial and well-being balance requires lifelong decision-making and deliberate work. This balance needs to be achieved for long-term success, enjoyment, and health. People can achieve a harmonious balance between money and well-being by establishing clear priorities, imposing boundaries, promoting wellness habits, adopting sound money management techniques, upholding strong relationships, and employing stress-reduction techniques. It's about integrating both into a happy and fulfilled existence, not about giving one priority over the other.

CONCLUSION: THIS IS YOUR UNPREDICTABLE MILLIONAIRE ADVENTURE

A priceless resource for information on creating and preserving wealth "Extraordinary Millionaire: Investment Tactics and Advice on How to Build and Preserve Wealth". Anyone who wants to take charge of their financial future and go on a journey towards financial achievement can find a thorough guide in the book. It provides readers with the information and abilities needed to make wise financial decisions by thoroughly examining investing strategies.

The book advises readers to look into a range of investing opportunities, including real estate, stock market investments, entrepreneurship, and more. It also highlights how important it is to maintain a broad financial portfolio. It highlights how important it is to have a growth mindset when pursuing wealth, to make specific financial objectives, to be patient and persistent, and to figure out what one's role in life is.

The book also emphasizes how crucial it is to match one's financial objectives with one's views and values and how crucial it is to make ethical and sustainable investments in today's society. It advances the notion that preserving wealth entails leading a sustainable, balanced life, fostering relationships with others, and preserving one's general health in addition to obtaining financial success.

In "Extraordinary Millionaire," readers will find a wealth of doable strategies, time-tested advice, and investment techniques to aid them in navigating the difficult world of finance. They discover the value of continuous learning and self-improvement, and they come to understand that human development is equally as significant as societal advancement.

In the end, this book is a guide for everyone who wants to accumulate and protect riches while keeping an all-encompassing outlook on life. It serves as a reminder that obtaining amazing riches is not the only way to live a meaningful life. Prioritizing relationships, personal fulfillment, and making a positive impact in the world is just as vital.

Readers may take charge of their financial future, make wise investment decisions, and make sure their money is passed down to future generations by using the information on these pages. "Extraordinary Millionaire" is an invaluable resource for everyone who wants to achieve amazing success in life—not just monetarily. It provides a thorough road map for earning and holding onto money while leading a contented, well-rounded life. Its pages include wisdom that goes far beyond financial achievement, touching on fundamental ideas that impact both financial prosperity and personal well-being.

One of the main points of the book is that having money is not a goal in and of itself, but rather a means to a happier and more meaningful existence. The author stresses the significance of having specific financial goals that go beyond merely amassing enormous wealth and instead entail creating a financial strategy that is in line with one's values and preferences. It is recommended that readers choose a wealth-building path that is both gratifying and in line with their life's purpose by combining financial goals with personal convictions.

Readers will learn about a wide range of investment strategies throughout the book, from conventional approaches to cutting-edge choices like sustainable investing and passive income streams. With so many options available to them, investors can select investing paths that align with their objectives, interests, and risk tolerance.

One of the book's main themes is the idea of sustainable and ethical investing. The author emphasizes that having wealth should be a reflection of one's morals rather than a means of compromising them. People can accumulate wealth and make a good impact on the environment and society by investing in businesses and projects that uphold moral and sustainable principles.

The book goes into deeper detail on the idea of wealth preservation, highlighting the fact that the long-term sustainability of wealth is just as important to financial success as its growth. It offers a structure for reducing risk, safeguarding assets, and preserving money for the next generations.

The significance of ongoing education and self-improvement is a recurrent theme throughout the book. The author highlights that true wealth includes not only material prosperity but also growth on a personal level, emotional stability, and intellectual advancement. It exhorts readers to adopt a growth mindset, look for learning opportunities, and establish recurring goals for themselves so they can adapt and change in an ever-changing world.

Throughout the book, there is also an emphasis on how important it is to live a balanced existence. It emphasizes the notion that monetary wealth shouldn't come at the expense of contentment and human connections. Rather, it promotes setting up boundaries, planning self-care, and creating strong relationships as necessary for leading a happy and satisfying life.

"Extraordinary Millionaire" offers a comprehensive approach to accumulating and protecting wealth. It goes above and beyond conventional financial advice by highlighting the need to live a balanced lifestyle, pursuing lifelong learning, and coordinating financial objectives with moral principles. The book provides readers with the information, tactics, and discernment needed to prioritize their general well-being while making wise financial decisions. It serves as a reminder that building a rich and meaningful life that is in line with one's core values and objectives is just as important to obtaining tremendous wealth as financial success.

MONTHLY BUDGET DIARY

MONTHLY PLANNER

Month:

Year:

SUN	MON	TUE	WED	THU	FRI	SAT

TOP PRIORITIES

ACHIEVEMENTS

EXPENDITURE

NOTES

MONTHLY PLANNER

Month:

Year:

SUN	MON	TUE	WED	THU	FRI	SAT

TOP PRIORITIES

ACHIEVEMENTS

EXPENDITURE

NOTES

MONTHLY PLANNER

Month:

Year:

SUN	MON	TUE	WED	THU	FRI	SAT

TOP PRIORITIES

ACHIEVEMENTS

EXPENDITURE

NOTES

MONTHLY PLANNER

Month:

Year:

SUN	MON	TUE	WED	THU	FRI	SAT

TOP PRIORITIES

ACHIEVEMENTS

EXPENDITURE

NOTES

MONTHLY PLANNER

Month:

Year:

SUN	MON	TUE	WED	THU	FRI	SAT

TOP PRIORITIES

ACHIEVEMENTS

EXPENDITURE

NOTES

MONTHLY PLANNER

Month:

Year:

SUN	MON	TUE	WED	THU	FRI	SAT

TOP PRIORITIES

ACHIEVEMENTS

EXPENDITURE

NOTES

MONTHLY PLANNER

Month:

Year:

SUN	MON	TUE	WED	THU	FRI	SAT

TOP PRIORITIES

ACHIEVEMENTS

EXPENDITURE

NOTES

MONTHLY PLANNER

Month:

Year:

SUN	MON	TUE	WED	THU	FRI	SAT

TOP PRIORITIES

ACHIEVEMENTS

EXPENDITURE

NOTES

MONTHLY PLANNER

Month:

Year:

SUN	MON	TUE	WED	THU	FRI	SAT

TOP PRIORITIES

ACHIEVEMENTS

EXPENDITURE

NOTES

MONTHLY PLANNER

Month:

Year:

SUN	MON	TUE	WED	THU	FRI	SAT

TOP PRIORITIES

ACHIEVEMENTS

EXPENDITURE

NOTES

MONTHLY PLANNER

Month:

Year:

SUN	MON	TUE	WED	THU	FRI	SAT

TOP PRIORITIES

ACHIEVEMENTS

EXPENDITURE

NOTES

MONTHLY PLANNER

Month:

Year:

SUN	MON	TUE	WED	THU	FRI	SAT

TOP PRIORITIES

ACHIEVEMENTS

EXPENDITURE

NOTES

MONTHLY PLANNER

Month:
Year:

SUN	MON	TUE	WED	THU	FRI	SAT

TOP PRIORITIES

ACHIEVEMENTS

EXPENDITURE

NOTES

MONTHLY PLANNER

Month:

Year:

SUN	MON	TUE	WED	THU	FRI	SAT

TOP PRIORITIES

ACHIEVEMENTS

EXPENDITURE

NOTES

MONTHLY PLANNER

Month:

Year:

SUN	MON	TUE	WED	THU	FRI	SAT

TOP PRIORITIES

ACHIEVEMENTS

EXPENDITURE

NOTES

MONTHLY PLANNER

Month:

Year:

SUN	MON	TUE	WED	THU	FRI	SAT

TOP PRIORITIES

ACHIEVEMENTS

EXPENDITURE

NOTES

MONTHLY PLANNER

Month:

Year:

SUN	MON	TUE	WED	THU	FRI	SAT

TOP PRIORITIES

ACHIEVEMENTS

EXPENDITURE

NOTES

MONTHLY PLANNER

Month:

Year:

SUN	MON	TUE	WED	THU	FRI	SAT

TOP PRIORITIES

ACHIEVEMENTS

EXPENDITURE

NOTES

MONTHLY PLANNER

Month:

Year:

SUN	MON	TUE	WED	THU	FRI	SAT

TOP PRIORITIES

ACHIEVEMENTS

EXPENDITURE

NOTES

MONTHLY PLANNER

Month:

Year:

SUN	MON	TUE	WED	THU	FRI	SAT

TOP PRIORITIES

ACHIEVEMENTS

EXPENDITURE

NOTES

MONTHLY PLANNER

Month:

Year:

SUN	MON	TUE	WED	THU	FRI	SAT

TOP PRIORITIES

ACHIEVEMENTS

EXPENDITURE

NOTES

MONTHLY PLANNER

Month:

Year:

SUN	MON	TUE	WED	THU	FRI	SAT

TOP PRIORITIES

ACHIEVEMENTS

EXPENDITURE

NOTES

MONTHLY PLANNER

Month:

Year:

SUN	MON	TUE	WED	THU	FRI	SAT

TOP PRIORITIES

ACHIEVEMENTS

EXPENDITURE

NOTES

MONTHLY PLANNER

Month:

Year:

SUN	MON	TUE	WED	THU	FRI	SAT

TOP PRIORITIES

ACHIEVEMENTS

EXPENDITURE

NOTES

MONTHLY PLANNER

Month:

Year:

SUN	MON	TUE	WED	THU	FRI	SAT

TOP PRIORITIES

ACHIEVEMENTS

EXPENDITURE

NOTES